AMI

Wealth, Prosperity & Abundance
Positive Affirmations

Written by Amirah Bellamy

I AM Wealth, Prosperity, Abundance Positive Affirmations. Copyright © 2017 by Etheric Realms Inv., LLC. All Rights Reserved. Printed in the United States of America. No part of this book may be used or reproduced in any manner whatsoever without written permission except in the case of brief quotations embodied in critical articles or reviews. For information contact:

twenty6dimension@gmail.com

I AM Wealth, Prosperity, Abundance Positive Affirmations

is dedicated to the infinite acquisition of massive wealth.

Acknowledgments

I thank the divine essence within for being the grounding force that empowers me to continue in creative bliss.

Opening Remarks...

Congratulations!!!! If you have chosen to read this book it is most likely because you have decided that it is high time that you positively improve your life, specifically with regards to the health of your wealth and I couldn't agree more! For that reason, I am so excited that you have boldly taken this step toward doing just that! I know that you will be hugely successful and that you will absolutely improve and change your life for the better!

Let me just say from experience that reading affirmations, saying them aloud, <u>listening to them</u>, falling asleep to them and/or meditating with them are all *very* effective ways of changing your perspective of life. **For starters**, affirmations are a way to practice positive thinking and self empowerment. They convince you (of the truth) that you can achieve absolutely anything that you set out to achieve. Affirmations shift thoughts from less desirable ones to more desirable ones, which is ultimately the most healthy mental space that you can possibly be in.

The health of your mental space is key to your ability to manifest your desires because the power to manifest comes as a result of your keenly focusing on what it is you want. So often we are so keenly focused on all the things that we do **not** desire, which leads to the manifestation of one undesirable circumstance after another. However, you have the power to change that, which is where the power of affirmations comes in.

Affirmations cause you to focus keenly on the power of the words that you are reading, reciting or listening to. It is that focus which will later transform into awareness, which later transforms into manifested reality. For instance, if you are reading this book it is likely that you are dissatisfied with the financial health of your current situation. You are feeling a lack of abundance of the things that you desire and you just aren't feeling very prosperous.

Now I want you to forget about all of that and receive what I am about to share with you. Those self-defeating beliefs couldn't be further from the truth and once you begin reading the affirmations contained in this book you will agree.

The affirmations in this book *will* heighten your awareness of the abundance of wealth that is currently surrounding you and that is yours for the receiving. Not only will you become aware of the abundance around you, but you will develop a sense of appreciation for it. Then, before you know it you will begin to feel nudges of inspiration which will move your towards taking inspired actions. This will all be instrumental in your manifesting the life of your dreams!

It is truly just that simple. So enjoy the affirmations in this book and open yourself up to receive the *power* of the words so that they inspire you to forever change your thoughts, your mind and your life. You are so deserving of a life of abundance, prosperity and wealth. You are so deserving of all of the wonderful, beautiful gifts that the universe has in store for you. It is time for you to now open yourself up to receive it.

Read these affirmations over and over again. Read at least 10 to 20 of them a day and really become one with each word. In time you will realize a change for the better in your life. You will realize a change in your disposition toward wealth. You will realize that many of your desires concerning wealth, abundance and prosperity are already beginning to come true. Simply read, receive, expand and enjoy!

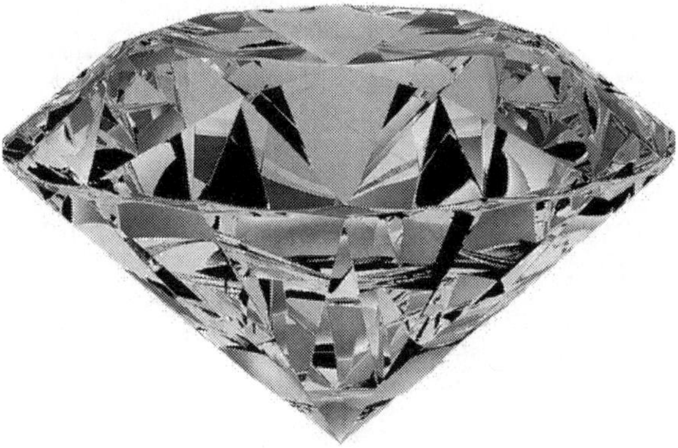

I am the synchronicity of prosperity manifested.
I am the essence of prosperous bliss.
I am the evidence of good intentions.
I am credible inspiration.
I am abundantly in the now.
All that I desire is within my reach.
I feel the bliss of financial wellness.
I am exceptionally adept at living well.
I am in good financial health.
Currency always finds its way to me.

I am enjoying the flow of the current of abundance.

I am the way to my bliss.

The current of prosperity transports me through life.

Every part of my being is one with prosperity.

I am one with the beat of the abundance of life.

I flow with the sea of passion.

I am the ease of faith.

I am headed in the direction of financial independence and freedom.

I am best known for honoring my financial commitments.

The pathway for financial abundance is now sexy enough for me to grace it with my presence.

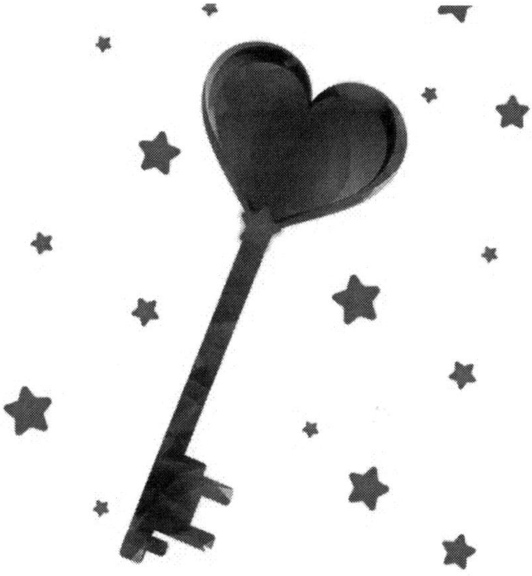

I approach life with grace and passion.
I am a creative genius at creating the wonderment of life.
I am connected to a euphoric way of life.
I am excellence.
My vision of joy is me.
I am happy to be in the presence of appreciation.
I am the dance partner of financial freedom performing in the world dance.
I know that I am meant to experience financial freedom.
My heart beats to the rhythm of prosperity.
I think financial freedom into existence.

I am the everything that is all of abundance.
I am overwhelmed by the emotion of allowing.
I am a choreography of infinite currency.
The river of currency naturally flows to my rhythm.
The power to thrive exists in me.
I am the will to push through life.
I am the thought to succeed manifested.
I am a dance away from bliss.
With every thought I am more financially liberated.
I feel the beat of an abundantly prosperous impulse.

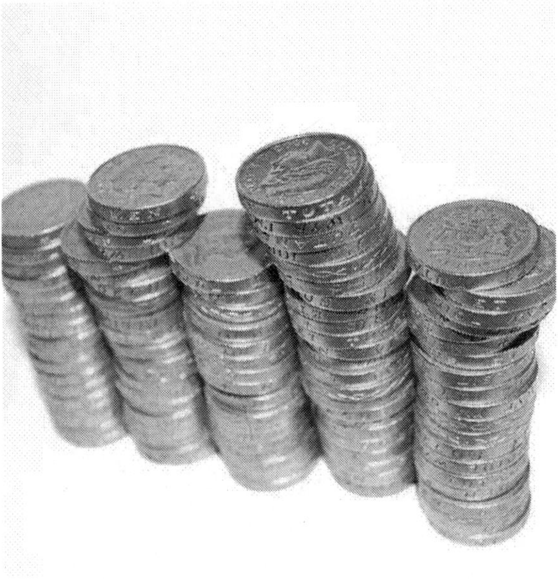

I am the music of a whimsical current.
I am the me that is suspended in a cloud of fiscal liberation.
I soar in the face of my expansion.
I am comfortable in my own radiant light..
I am a mythical truth of free-flowing currency.
I have given up everything to now live the dream of manifesting everything.
I am the fastest growing dream evolved.
I am fortified by currency and grounded in self-determination.
I am so rich with the abundance of now.
I am a wish come true for more.

I am within the scope of a bountiful future.
I am within the grasp of abundance.
I am in the range of opulence.
I am richness unchecked.
The vibration of currency dances to the rhythm of my drum.
I am engulfed in the many luxuries of wealth.
I am stalked by splendor.
I am the poshness of fine living.
At the heart of affluence is me.
I am the friend of diamonds, currency and life's treasures.

I am the dawn of a new current of wealth.
Every treasure is a part of me.
My ability to see the abstract is more valuable than gold.
I love the richness of life like it's all that I have.
I am partnered with the sweetness of life.
I am the first sight of love.
I am wealth to infinity.
I am an infusion of inspiration, zest and fascination with the thrill of life.
I am the link between will and manifestation.
I am naturally evolving into someone more grand.

Everywhere that I look abundance comes into my awareness.
I see the abundance of goodness in all things.
I am a favorable choice.
I am royal in all of my glory.
I am exciting to be around.
I am infectiously joyous.
Fortune is my natural companion.
The sure way to a bountiful existence is through me.
I am the kind of person that riches cling to.
I am goodness abound.

I am the crux of the reality of awesome.
My life is a series of profitable thoughts.
The teachable moments of life inspire my expansion.
I expect good things to happen.
My expectations manifest into my expansion.
Prosperity is sacred to my existence.
I am intoxicated with wealth.
I am the start of something wonderful.
My journey to wealth began with a grand thought.
I am living a dream.

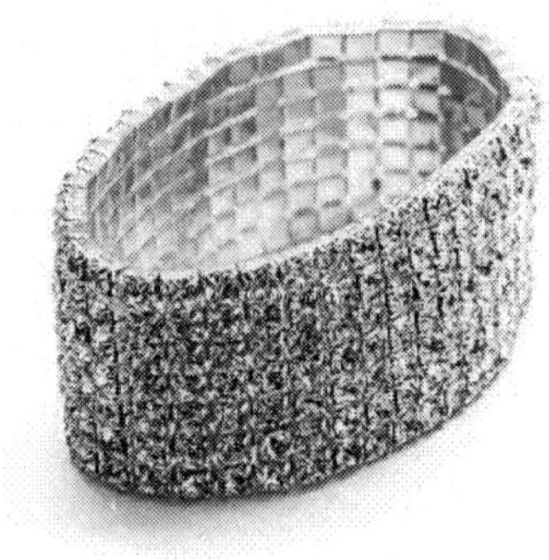

The operative progression of riches begins at my point of focus.
My point of focus is always on my expansion.
The part of me that excels is exponentially satisfied.
I am a decided plan for success.
I am the creator of the good in my life.
I am flourishing into an affirmed state of being.
I am adjoined at the heart to affluence.
I enjoy every moment of my life as a lavish experience.
All of my needs are fulfilled.
I am at the center of a wonderful life.

I am fulfilled to capacity.
I am drunken with wealth.
I am a prolific force of prosperity.
Anything that matches my taste matches my wealth.
I am ready for abundance.
Prosperity is now convenient for me.
I am the finest consort of life.
I am a reflection of my prosperous thoughts.
Those who see me see an abundance of wealth.
My networth rivals the richest among me.

I am constantly on the receiving end of opportunities.
I am the inspiration of my life work of art.
The bliss of living comes easy to me.
I am in the best financial shape of my life.
I am an exclusive.
I am steadily making progress on the path toward wealth.
I am a profitable investment worth the risk.
I am authentically fabulous.
I am effortlessly drawn to wealth,
All of the ingredients of wealth naturally occur in me.

I wear the gorgeous glow of wealth with pride.
I am a safe haven for prosperity to settle.
I come from a long line of wealth.
I am genetically predispositioned to live a life of wealth.
Like the river of life prosperity flows with me.
I am of the mind of wealth.
Wealth multiplies times itself in my bank account.
I am always brought to a state of joy when I think about my wealth.
I am expensive taste.
I am a state of appreciation.

I am going to the ends of the earth in wealth.
I live, breath and sleep the prosperity of my being.
I am as happy as I can be in wealth.
I am the loveliest wealth charm.
I am a richness likened to satin.
I celebrate my success in all that I do.
I want more so I expect more.
I am extremely wealthy.
Wealth keeps me connected to the best of who I am.
I am classically trained in wealth.

I am full of smiles, hopefulness and wealth.
I am a newly acquired treasure.
I am a fancy term for rich.
I am a sleek, healthy option for expansion.
I am steeped in wealth to perfection.
A lot of wealth balances me out.
Those who know me love me in abundance.
I am the kind of person that successful people cling to.
I am in a word richness.
I am state of the art.

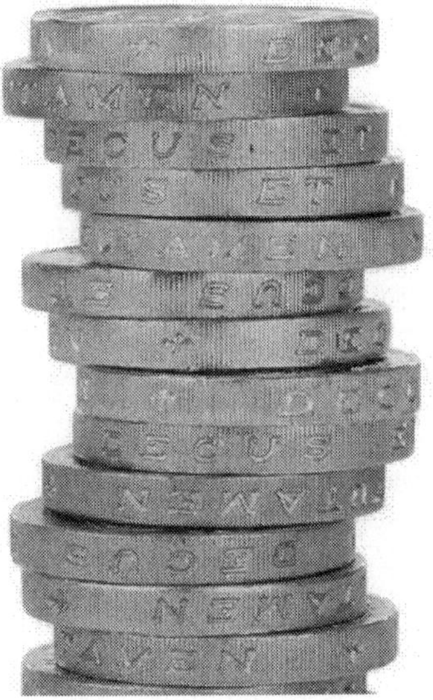

I am the manifestation of abundance.
I am prosperous.
I am on track to obtain massive wealth.
I am a magnet for the riches of the world.
I am the manifestation of all of my desires.
I am in alignment with all that I desire.
I am a divine prosperous being.
I am the source of the abundance that I seek.
I am all of my dreams come true.
I am the vibration of success.

I am blissfully satisfied.
I am the cause of great success.
I am an admirable success story.
I am the outcome of endless possibilities.
I am the light on the path to life's treasure.
I am the melody of prosperous resonance.
I am the paragon of abundance.
I am the destination of the natural flow of prosperity.
I am in full control of my life.
I am able to acquire anything that I want.

I am always drawn to wealth.
I am my greatest opportunity.
I am feeling good about what I have accomplished.
I am the way to my own success.
I am one with universal abundance.
I am deserving of the finer things in life.
I am deserving of all that I desire.
I am deserving of a wealthy lifestyle.
I am deserving of the best that life has to offer.
I am the best that life has to offer.

I am abundance.
I am bliss.
I am happiness.
I am ultimate satisfaction.
I am the best of all that is good.
I am a spark of inspiration.
I am a powerful testimony.
I am a feel good thought.
I am the creator of my destiny
and I am destined for greatness.

I am living my moment of truth.
I am living in the lap of luxury.
I am living in harmony with my higher self.
I am living my dreams.
I am living.
I am exuberant.
I am enjoying life's journey.
I am a beautiful journey.
I am a spirit of abundance.
I am prosperous from the inside out.

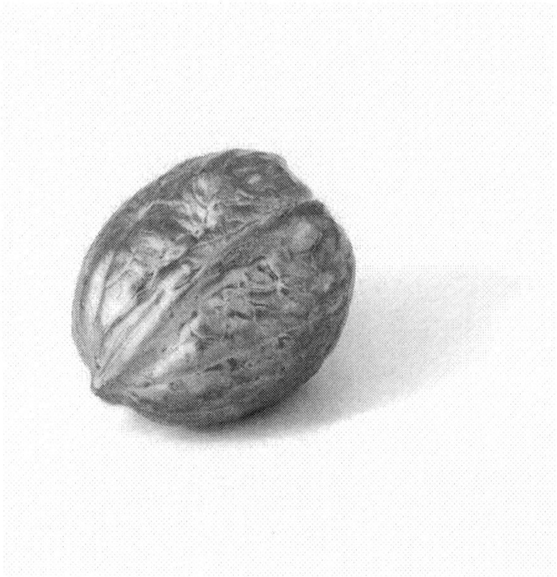

I am a most expanded form of wealth.
I am always expanding.
I am always evolving.
I am always improving.
I am always becoming more than I am.
I am always in a natural state of being my best self.
I am always prosperous.
I am everything that is prosperous.
I am constantly reaching new heights.
I am a traveler of prosperous realities.

I am all that I need.
I am conducive to my well-being.
I am an original version of me.
I am a master of wealth.
I am in a good relationship with money.
I am my biggest fan.
I am expectant of good things.
I am confident in all that I am.
I am the maker of my success.
I am a winner.

I am so excited about what good will come.
I am so ecstatic about the wealth that surrounds me.
I am so free.
I am so rich with goodness.
I am so happy to breath in the goodness of life.
I am in awe of my life.
I am a good fit for wealth.
I am a vibrational match for abundance.
I am the soulmate of prosperity.
I am in the mood for wealth.

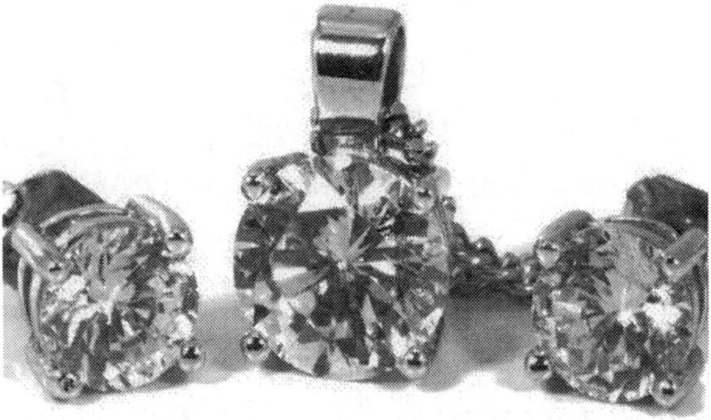

I am living more than I could ever dream.
I am fine-tuned with wealth.
I am the masterpiece of prosperity.
I am the mind of richness.
I am the now.
I am the present of desire.
I am the manifestor of wishes.
I am the intention of my best day.
I am appreciation manifested.
I am wildly fascinated with success.

I am a magnet for great opportunities.
I am in the vortex of greatness.
I am the home of wealth.
I am free to be all that I aspire to be.
I am a capsule of greatness ready to expand.
I am my greatest surprise.
I am luxurious.
I am a poetic stance.
I am elegantly esteemed.
I am royal.

I am highly regarded.
I am honored.
I am regal.
I am the glory of time.
I am empowered.
I am enjoying the process of my evolution.
I am beautiful.
I am a pleasure to all the senses.
I am abundantly vibrant.
I am abundant in every aspect of my being.

I am the transformer of circumstances.
I am electrifying.
I am the pulse of wealth.
I am the good in everything.
I am the top of the line.
I am high end.
I am notoriously rich.
I am classic.
I am fine dining.
I am elegance.

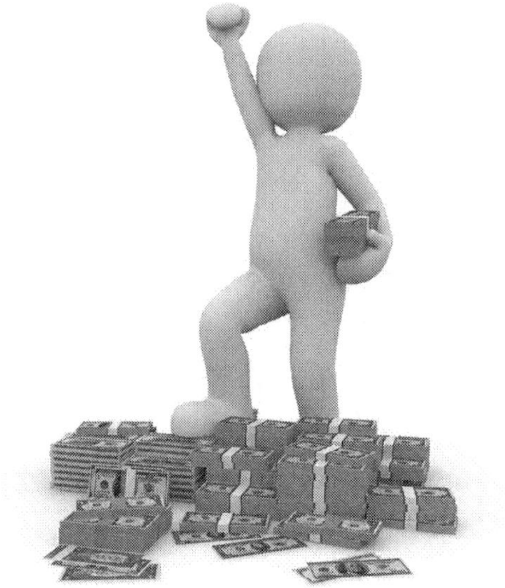

I am the upper echelon.
I am infinite bliss.
I am stylish.
I am more than greatness.
I am a power source.
I am flourishing change.
I am the mind's wealth champion.
I am the eye of destiny.
I am the ear of the wonderful richness of life's voice.
I am the spirit of opulence.

I am a source of abundance.
I am a wealth of knowledge.
I am infinitely prosperous.
I am a magnet for wealth.
I am drawn to fine living.
I am confident about the success of my future.
I am adorned in the richness of life.
I am a priceless refreshing experience.
I am fascinated with my ability to amass wealth.
I am all that I need.

I am free to thrive.
I am living proof that dreams do come true.
I am the evidence of success.
I am a vessel of prosperity.
I am harmoniously aligned with wealth.
Money comes easily to me.
I am exactly where I am supposed to be.
Each day my life gets better.
I am a vibrational match to all that I desire.
I am the recipient of all the luxuries in life.

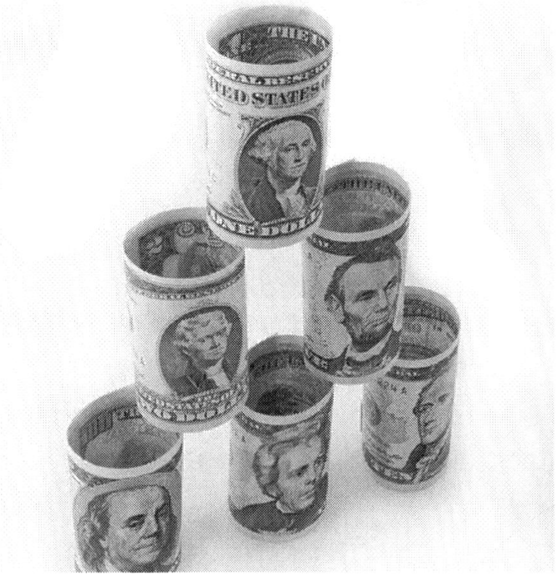

I am divine wisdom.
I am my most sure bet.
I am so focused on what I most desire.
I am so aligned with my truth.
I am so confident in my ability to manifest my dreams.
I am a dream maker.
I am a prodigy of my divine destiny.
Whatever I desire I manifest.
I am the best part of the feeling of life.
I am tuned in to the frequency of wealth.

I am very aware of my ability to create wealth.
I am an amazing creation.
I am the causer of the wonder in my life.
I am in control of my destiny.
I am a being of prosperity.
I have amassed an abundance of wealth.
I am living consciousness of wonderment.
I am one with my divine essence.
I am a manifestor of great things.
I am the frequency of wealth.

I am the feeling of abundance.
I am consciously creating multiple streams of wealth.
I am a measurement of wealth consciousness that is infinite.
I am allowing abundance into my life.
I am the evidence of my financial progress.
I am prosperity manifested.
I am wealth manifested.
I am abundance manifested.
I am enjoying the process of my expansion.
I am enjoying the goodness of my bliss.

54

I am the abundance of all goodness.
The abundance of wealth is all around me.
I am the beauty in all things.
I am the one who is abundantly spectacular.
I am focused on what I want.
I am my own kind of beautiful.
I am the epitome of good things.
I am a constant source of inspiration.
I am abundantly fulfilled.
I am the beginning of an endless stream of wealth.

I am flowing with the current of prosperity.
I am persistently prosperous.
I am the offspring of prosperity and wealth.
I am free to be as wealthy as I want to be.
I am the river of abundance and I flow.
I am looking forward to the abundance of wonderful things to come.
I am so sure of my success.
I am so present in this moment of assurance of my ability to create the life of my dreams.
I am creating paradise with every thought.
I am focused on creating something that feels so deliciously grand.

I am exactly where I am supposed to be.
I am in awe of my creations.

I am a decadent flavor of a divine manifestation.
I live a decadently rich lifestyle.
I am an omnipotent power.
I am a dream come true.
I am a work of art.
I am priceless.
I am evolving into greatness.
I am consistently prosperous.

The wealth that I desire is within my reach.
I am focused only on what matters most, my true desires.
I am happy about the life that I have created.
I am proud of what I have achieved.
I am the richness of life.
I am the creator of beautiful things.
I am the wonderment of life.
I am conscious abundance.
I am conscious prosperity.
I am conscious wealth.

I am what I want.
I am the feeling of richness and abundance.
I am a flowing stream of love and abundance.
I am in the gravitational pull of wealth.
I am where it feels good to be.
I am prime and divine.
I am an elegant model design.
I am enriched paradise.
I am a well thought out plan.
All that I desire manifests for me.

I am a vision of wealth.
I am wealth realized.
I am the best part of life.
I am airborne and free to be me.
I am abundantly living the life of my dreams.
I am consumed with the richness of who I am.
I am a beautiful desire.
I am a beautiful vision.
I am an original masterpiece.
I am so inspired to manifest abundance.

I am so inspired by what I have already manifested.
I am so inspired by me.
I am happy to be inspired.
I am happy to be living.
I am living a wonderful dream.
Wealth lays a well-laid path for me.
Prosperity lights my way.
I am mindfully aware of abundance.
I am attuned to the frequency of prosperity.
I am attuned to the frequency of wealth.

I am attuned to the frequency of abundance.
I am a creator of massive wealth.
Wealth comes to me from multiple sources.
Wealth comes to me easily.
I am a free-flowing current of wealth.
I expand always in all ways.
I am at the center of fortune.
I am a resource of massive riches.
I am a being of substance.
I am high quality.

64

I am a person of wealth.
Cash is drawn to me.
I am a spectacular view.
I am infinitely expanding.
My intention to expand is definite.
I am at the crux of something phenomenal.
I am quickly approaching affluence.
I am in possession of large amounts of money.
I am financially intelligent.
I am financially educated.

I am in a state of being rich.
I am an abundance of valuable riches.
I am in a state of affluence.
I am happy and prosperous.
I am in a state of spiritual well-being.
I am a wealth creator.
I have multiple streams of income.
I am living a lavish lifestyle.
I am generous and kind.
I am generously given to abundance.

I naturally gravitate toward prosperity and wealth.
I am among the super rich.
I am a warm-spirited prosperous being.
I am flourishing financially.
I am vigorously fortunate.
I am financially successful.
I am at the point of focus of prosperity.
I am agreeable to fortune.
I am a successful, flourishing, thriving being.
I am rising to greatness.

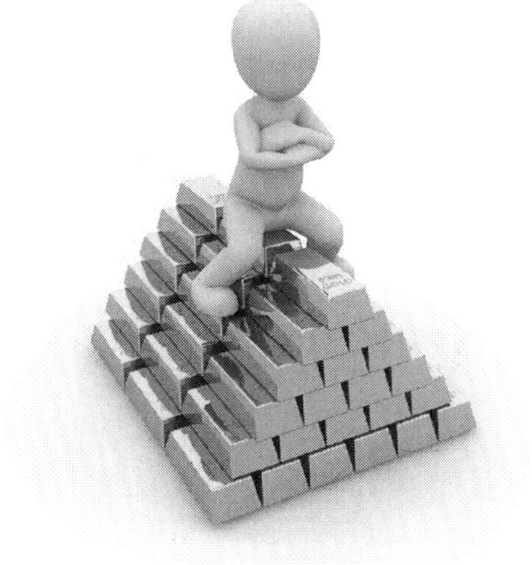

I am advancing in the pursuit of my desires.
I am marked by peace and prosperity.
The bounty of fortune surrounds me.
The fortune of the future is my destined path.
I am draped in the richness of my rich existence.
I am loyal to my highest self.
I am free to live prosperously.
I am the bliss of richness.
I am the window of the soul of divinity.
I am one with richness.

I am committed to the acquisition of wealth.
I am committed to the expansion of my higher self.
I am opened to the abundance of love.
I am opened to the abundance of life.
I am the doorway to an abundant future.
I am intimately linked to fortune.
I am a treasure to behold.
I am a valuable asset.
I am blinded by the light of my rich future.
I am secure in my ability to amass great wealth.

I am successful in all things.
I am the truth of prosperity.
I am bound to a life of wealth.
The lavishness of life embraces me.
I am caressed by the hand of fortune.
I am loving the richness of every
moment of my life.
I am enjoying the joy in my life.
I am floating on a cloud of happiness.
I am the goodness of time.
I am joyfully bound to abundance.

I have a sacred connection to fine living.
I have a fondness for fine things.
Fortune claims my life.
I am seduced by the beauty of life.
I am prepared for the realization of wealth.
I am worthy of the best that life has to offer.
I am willingly under the spell of good living.
I am prepared for good things to happen.
I am wealth inspired.
I am the realization of prosperity.

I am the pinnacle of an abundant journey.
I am the heart and soul of wealth and goodness.
I am the beauty of the fullness of a wealth-inspired life.
I am the divine inspiration to prosper.
I am in love with money and the freedom that it brings.
Where I go abundance flows.
I am flourishing in the richness of my divine wealth.
I am the goodness that happens in life.
I am the infinity of richness.
I am tapped into the infinite universal abundance.

I magnetically attract to me the infinite prosperity of the universe.
I am certain of the manifestation of abundance in my life.
I am proof that wealth is infinite.
I am sublimely linked to wealth.
I am the sweetness of victory.
I am compelled to live a life of abundance.
I am draped in the power of opulence.
I am a supreme source of wealth.
I am an eternal stream of prosperity.
I am everything that I should be and more.

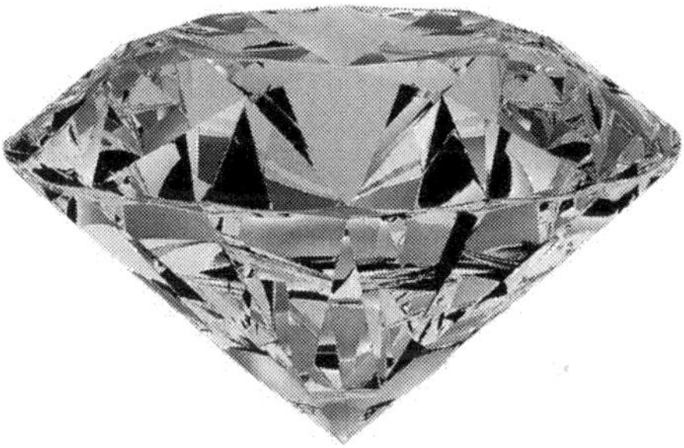

I hope that the positive affirmations in this book were a healing, fulfilling medicine for your soul and that they in some way enriched your life. With that I wish you a life of wealth, prosperity, abundance and a more blissful vision of the world.

Exist purely in love!

If you enjoyed this book or received value from it in any way, then I'd like to ask you for a favor. Would you be kind enough to leave a review for this book on Amazon? It'd be greatly appreciated!

About the Author...

Amirah Bellamy is the Executive Board Chair of Life Arts Institute. She has a BS and MA in Counseling Psychology. She's also an artist of many crafts. She's been a writer for over 19 years, a yogi for over 10 years, a singer for over 15 years, nutritionista for over 16 years and has thoroughly enjoyed being mom to 2 beautiful children.

To learn more about Amirah Bellamy

visit….. www.EthericRealmsInv.com

Other books by this author....

The Gift: *Sacral Chakra*	**The Gift:** *Solar Plexus Chakra*
The Gift: *Heart Chakra*	**The Gift:** *Throat Chakra*

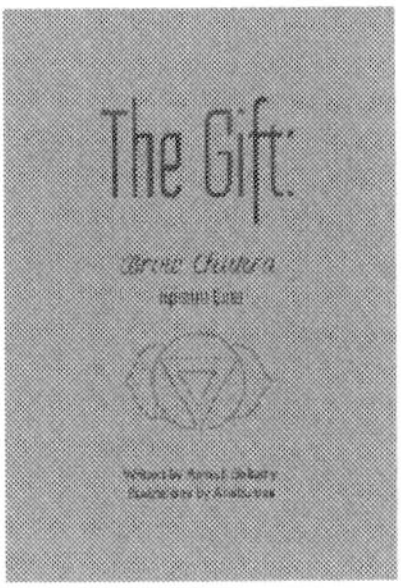
The Gift:

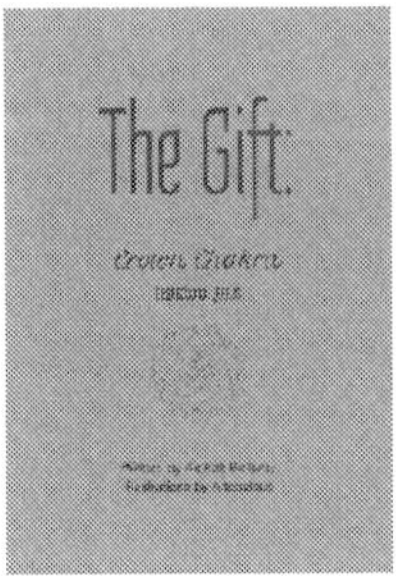
The Gift: